S0-AHU-105

DISASTERS IN HISTORY

THE Apollo 13 MISSION

by Donald B. Lemke
illustrated by Keith Tucker

Consultant:
James Gerard
Aerospace Education Specialist
Kennedy Space Center

Capstone press

Mankato, Minnesota

Graphic Library is published by Capstone Press,
1710 Roe Crest Drive, North Mankato, Minnesota 56003.
www.capstonepub.com

Library of Congress Cataloging-in-Publication Data
Lemke, Donald B.
    The Apollo 13 mission / by Donald B. Lemke ; illustrated by Keith Tucker.
    p. cm.—(Graphic library. Disasters in history)
    Includes bibliographical references and index.
    ISBN-13: 978-0-7368-5476-4 (hardcover)   ISBN-10: 0-7368-5476-2 (hardcover)
    ISBN-13: 978-0-7368-6871-6 (softcover pbk.)   ISBN-10: 0-7368-6871-2 (softcover pbk.)
    1. Apollo 13 (Spacecraft)—Accidents—Juvenile literature. 2. Space vehicle accidents—United
States—Juvenile literature. I. Tucker, Keith. II. Title. III. Series.
TL789.8.U6L33 2006
629.45'4—dc22   2005028477

Summary: In graphic novel format, tells the dramatic story of the rescue of the Apollo 13
    astronauts.

Art Direction
Jason Knudson

Graphic Designers
Juliette Peters and Jason Knudson

Production Designer
Alison Thiele

Colorist
Kim Brown

Editor
Tom Adamson

Editor's note: Direct quotations from primary sources are indicated by a yellow background.

Direct quotations appear on the following pages:
Pages 5, 7, 9, 10, 11, 13, 23, 24, 25, 26, from Apollo 13 PAO Mission Commentary Transcript
    (http://www.jsc.nasa.gov/history/mission_trans/apollo13.htm).
Pages 14 (top panel), 15, 22, quoted in Failure Is Not an Option by Gene Kranz (New York:
    Simon & Schuster, 2000).
Pages 14 (bottom panel), 17, 19, 20, quoted in Lost Moon by Jim Lovell (Boston: Houghton
    Mifflin, 1994).

Printed in the United States of America in Stevens Point, Wisconsin.
042013
007323R

TABLE OF CONTENTS

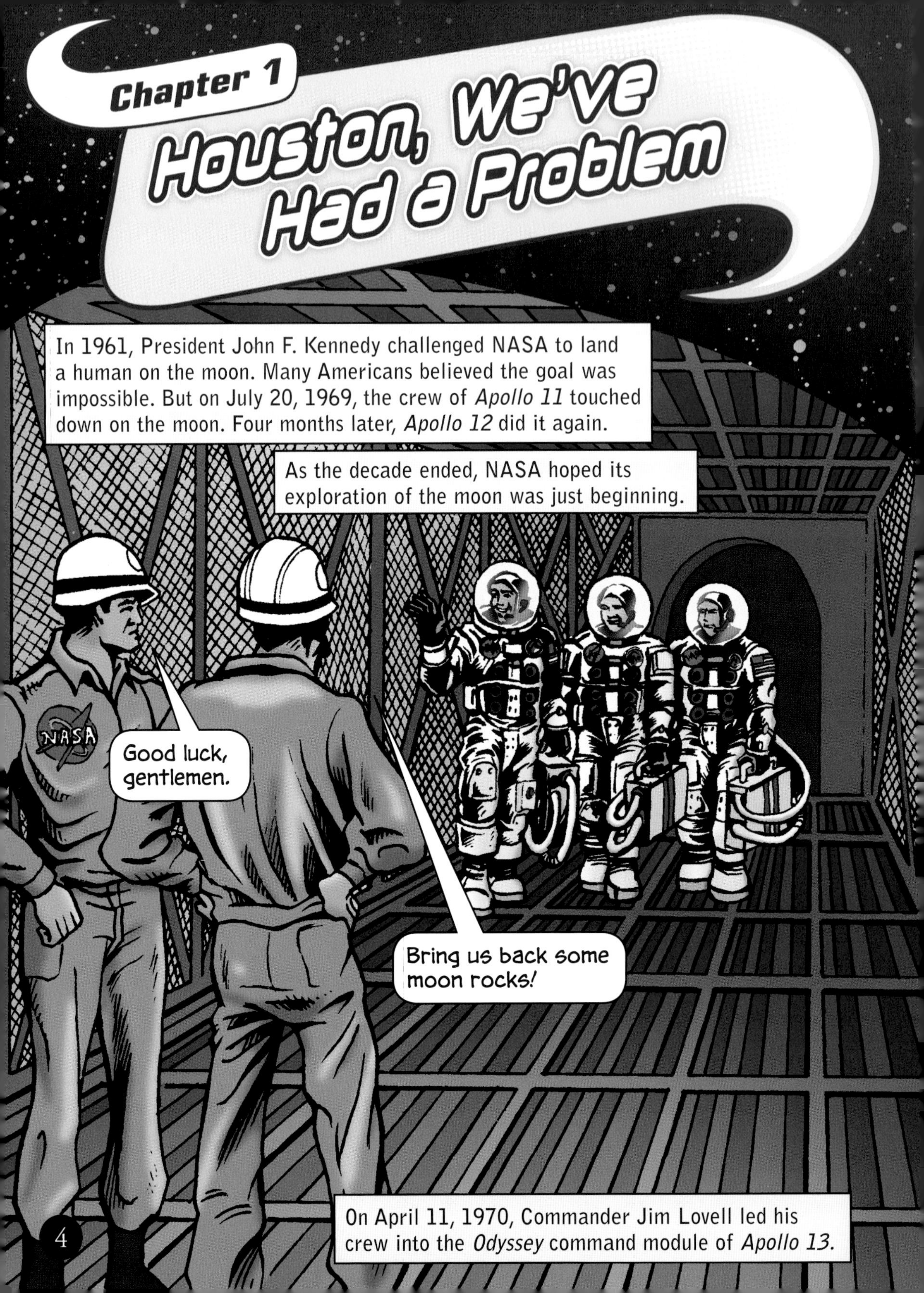
Chapter 1
Houston, We've Had a Problem
In 1961, President John F. Kennedy challenged NASA to land a human on the moon. Many Americans believed the goal was impossible. But on July 20, 1969, the crew of *Apollo 11* touched down on the moon. Four months later, *Apollo 12* did it again.
As the decade ended, NASA hoped its exploration of the moon was just beginning.
NASA
Good luck, gentlemen.
Bring us back some moon rocks!
On April 11, 1970, Commander Jim Lovell led his crew into the *Odyssey* command module of *Apollo 13*.

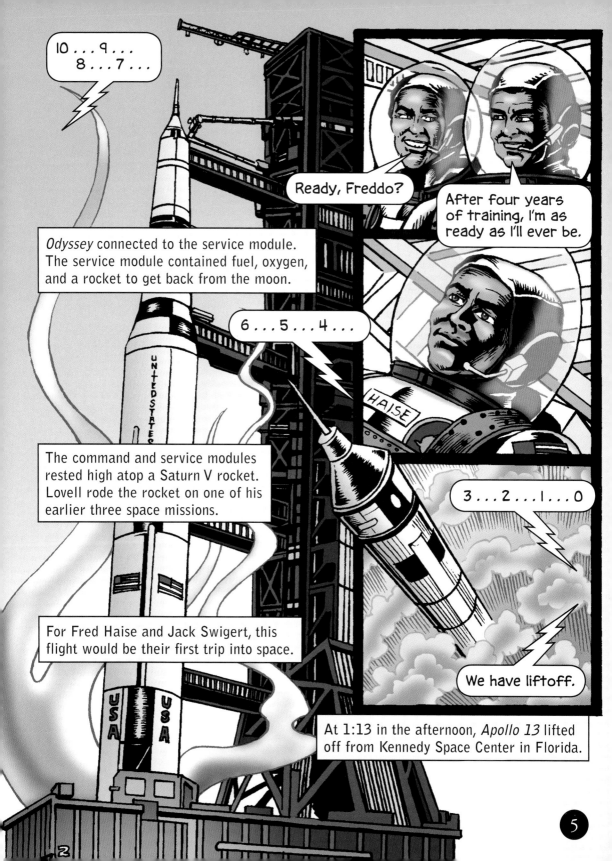

10 . . . 9 . . . 8 . . . 7 . . .

Ready, Freddo?

After four years of training, I'm as ready as I'll ever be.

Odyssey connected to the service module. The service module contained fuel, oxygen, and a rocket to get back from the moon.

6 . . . 5 . . . 4 . . .

The command and service modules rested high atop a Saturn V rocket. Lovell rode the rocket on one of his earlier three space missions.

3 . . . 2 . . . 1 . . . 0

For Fred Haise and Jack Swigert, this flight would be their first trip into space.

We have liftoff.

At 1:13 in the afternoon, *Apollo 13* lifted off from Kennedy Space Center in Florida.

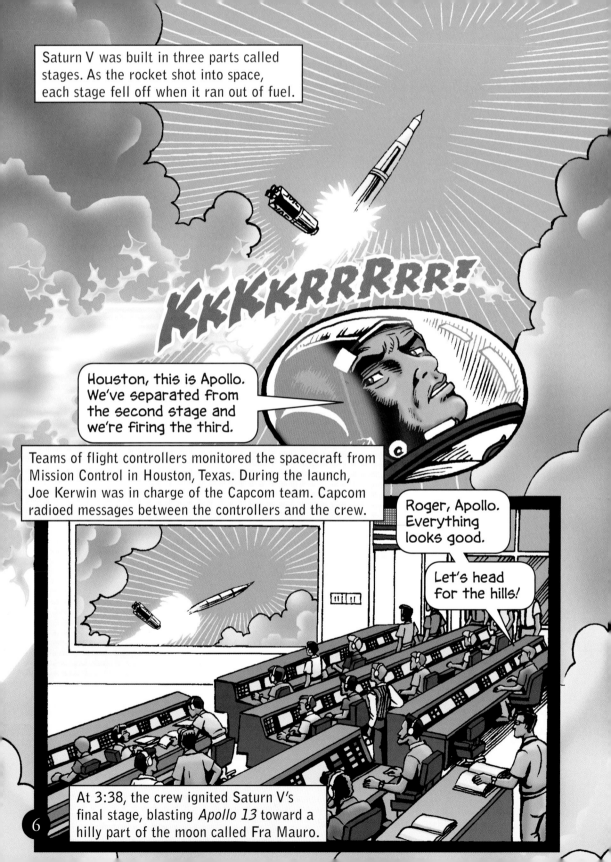

Saturn V was built in three parts called stages. As the rocket shot into space, each stage fell off when it ran out of fuel.

KKKKRRRRR!

Houston, this is Apollo. We've separated from the second stage and we're firing the third.

Teams of flight controllers monitored the spacecraft from Mission Control in Houston, Texas. During the launch, Joe Kerwin was in charge of the Capcom team. Capcom radioed messages between the controllers and the crew.

Roger, Apollo. Everything looks good.

Let's head for the hills!

At 3:38, the crew ignited Saturn V's final stage, blasting *Apollo 13* toward a hilly part of the moon called Fra Mauro.

6

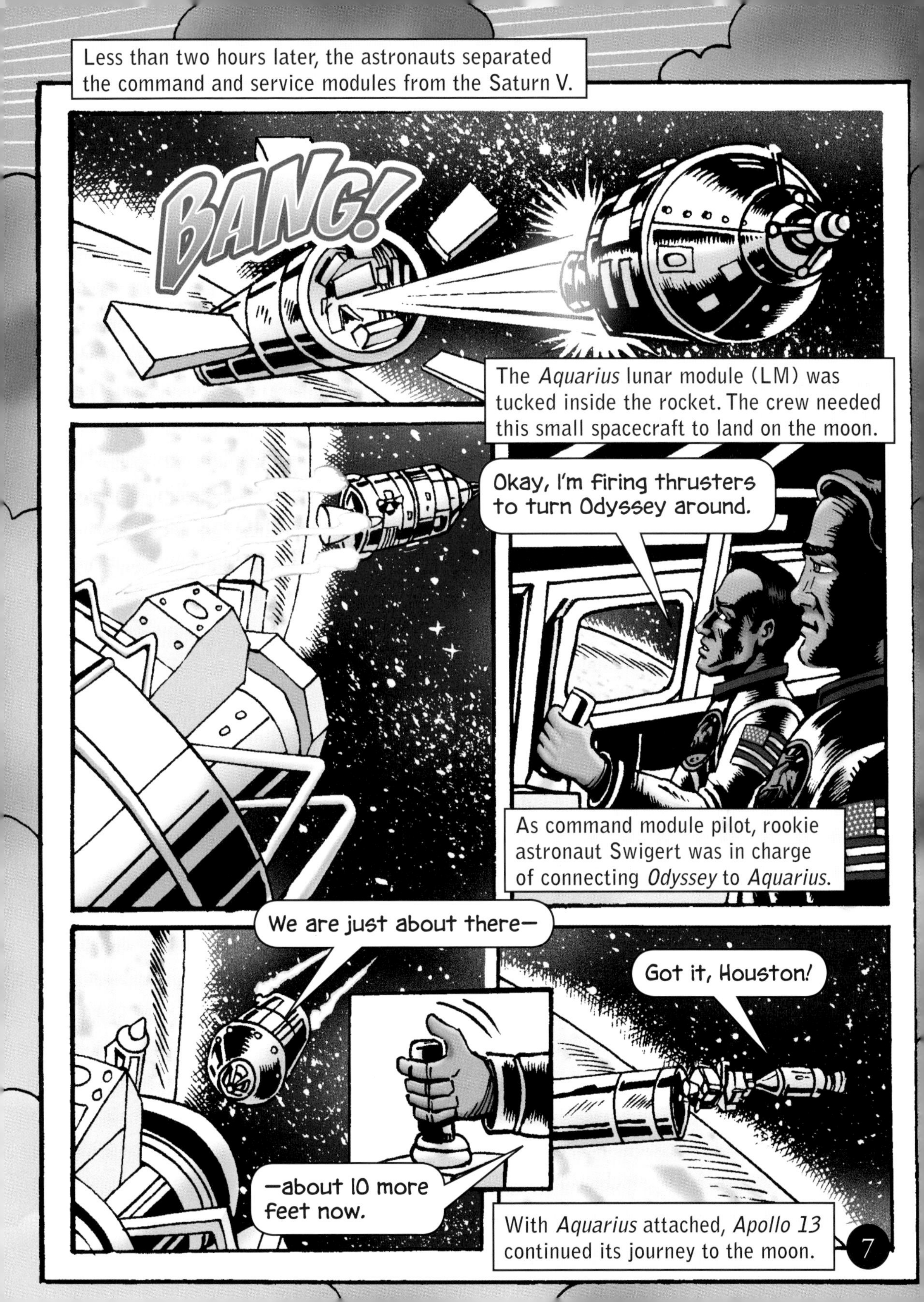
Less than two hours later, the astronauts separated the command and service modules from the Saturn V.
BANG!
The *Aquarius* lunar module (LM) was tucked inside the rocket. The crew needed this small spacecraft to land on the moon.
Okay, I'm firing thrusters to turn Odyssey around.
As command module pilot, rookie astronaut Swigert was in charge of connecting *Odyssey* to *Aquarius*.
We are just about there—
—about 10 more feet now.
Got it, Houston!
With *Aquarius* attached, *Apollo 13* continued its journey to the moon.

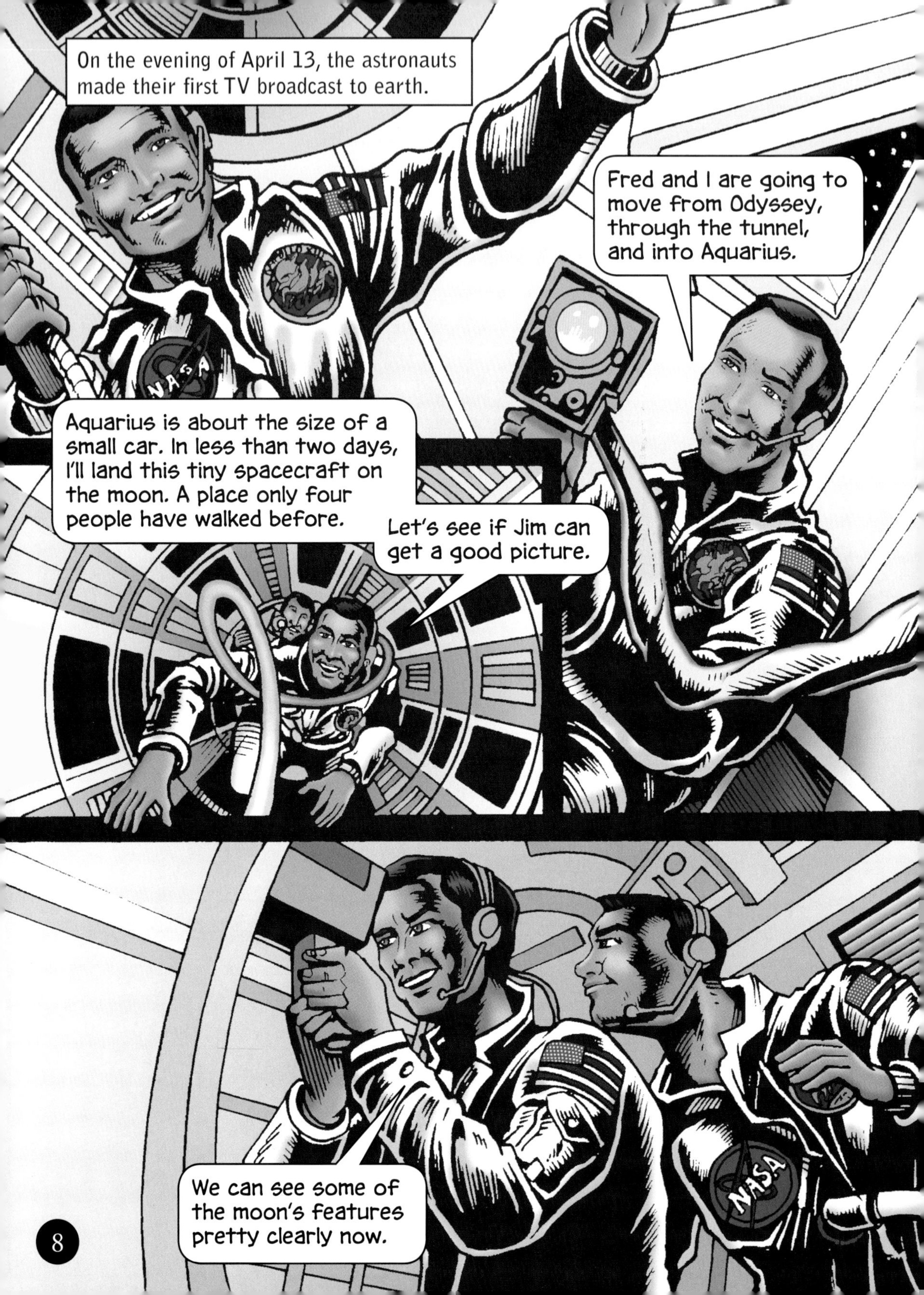
On the evening of April 13, the astronauts made their first TV broadcast to earth.
Fred and I are going to move from Odyssey, through the tunnel, and into Aquarius.
Aquarius is about the size of a small car. In less than two days, I'll land this tiny spacecraft on the moon. A place only four people have walked before.
Let's see if Jim can get a good picture.
We can see some of the moon's features pretty clearly now.

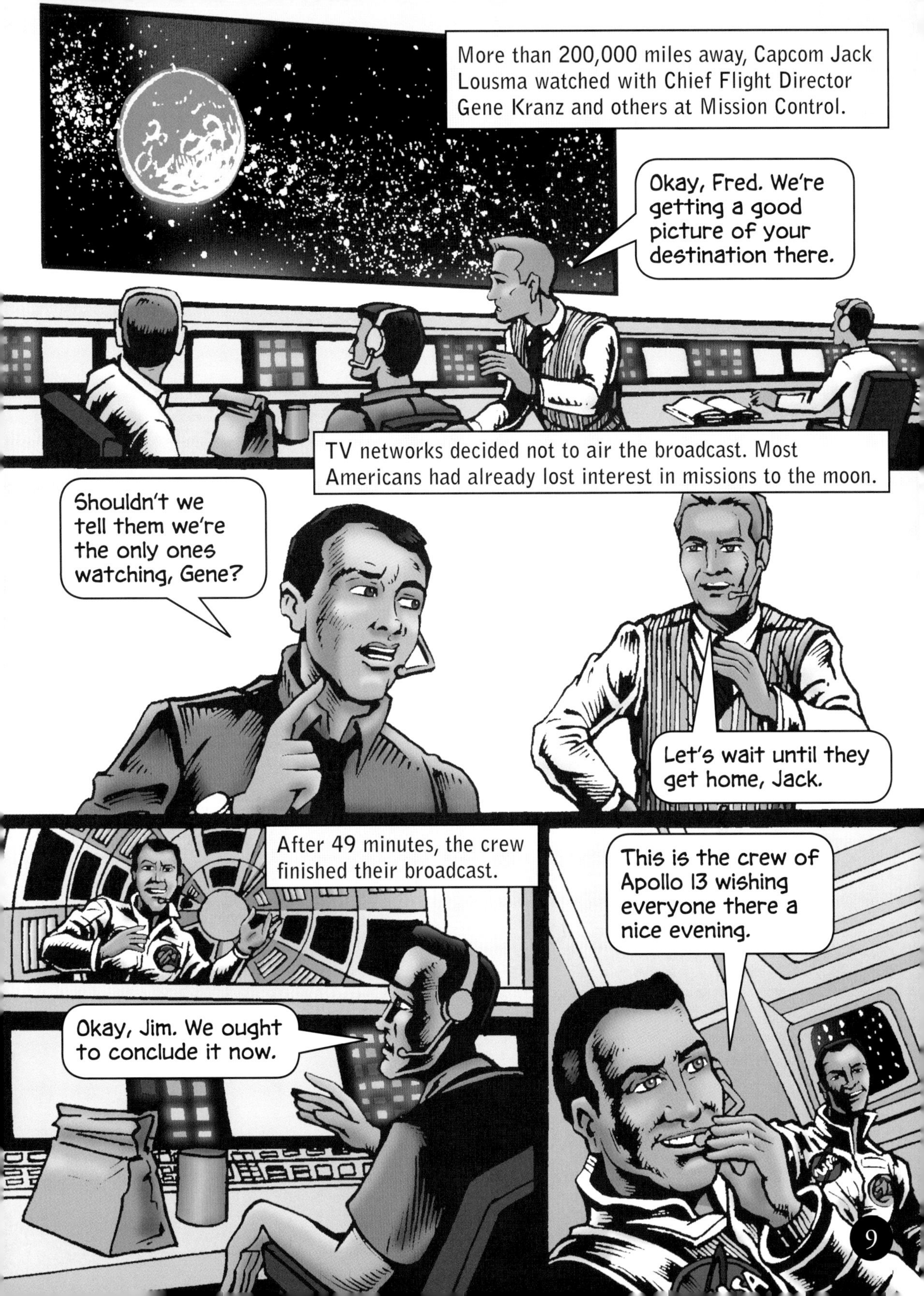
More than 200,000 miles away, Capcom Jack Lousma watched with Chief Flight Director Gene Kranz and others at Mission Control.
Okay, Fred. We're getting a good picture of your destination there.
TV networks decided not to air the broadcast. Most Americans had already lost interest in missions to the moon.
Shouldn't we tell them we're the only ones watching, Gene?
Let's wait until they get home, Jack.
After 49 minutes, the crew finished their broadcast.
Okay, Jim. We ought to conclude it now.
This is the crew of Apollo 13 wishing everyone there a nice evening.

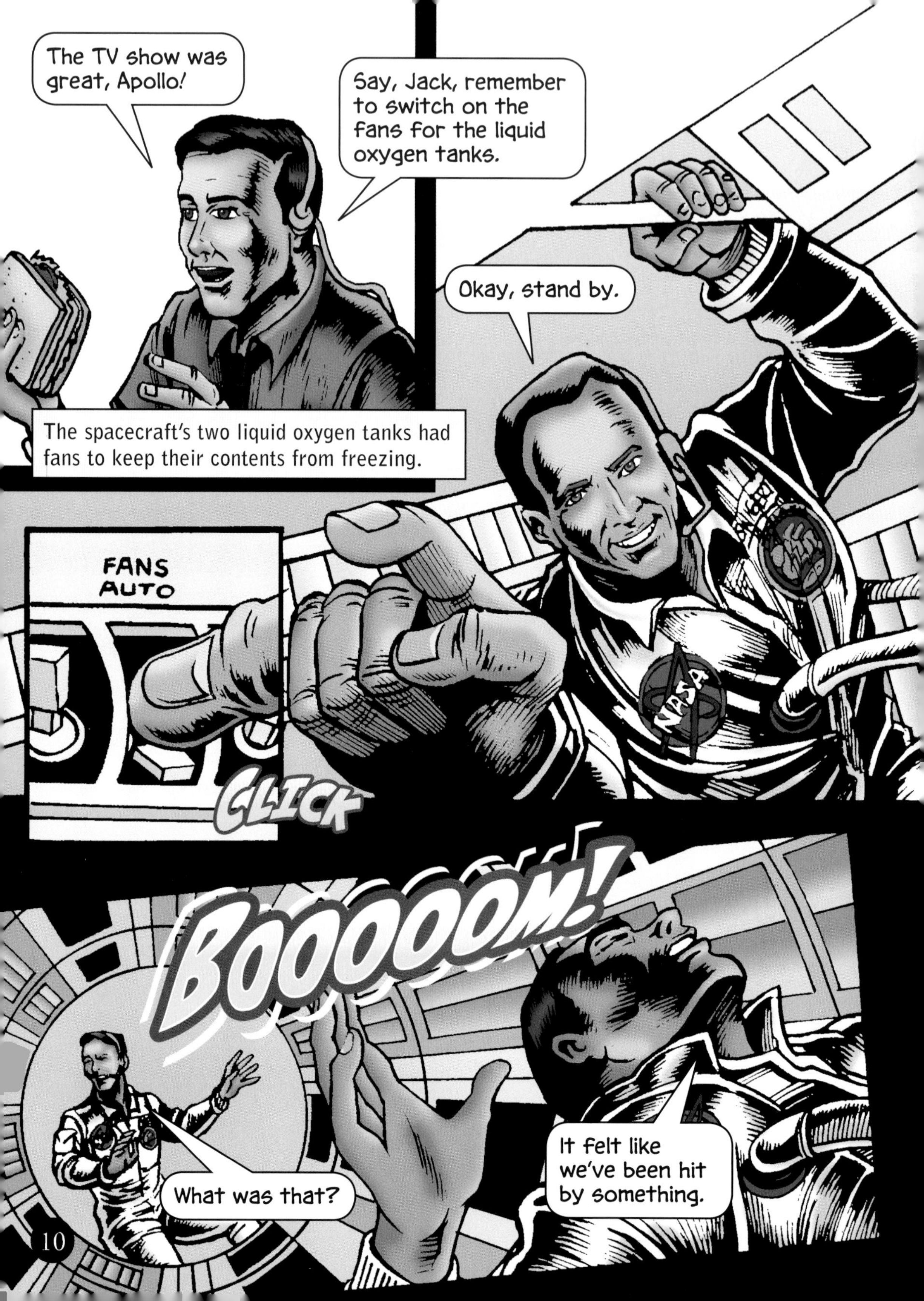
The TV show was great, Apollo!
Say, Jack, remember to switch on the fans for the liquid oxygen tanks.
The spacecraft's two liquid oxygen tanks had fans to keep their contents from freezing.
Okay, stand by.
FANS AUTO
CLICK
BOOOOOM!
What was that?
It felt like we've been hit by something.

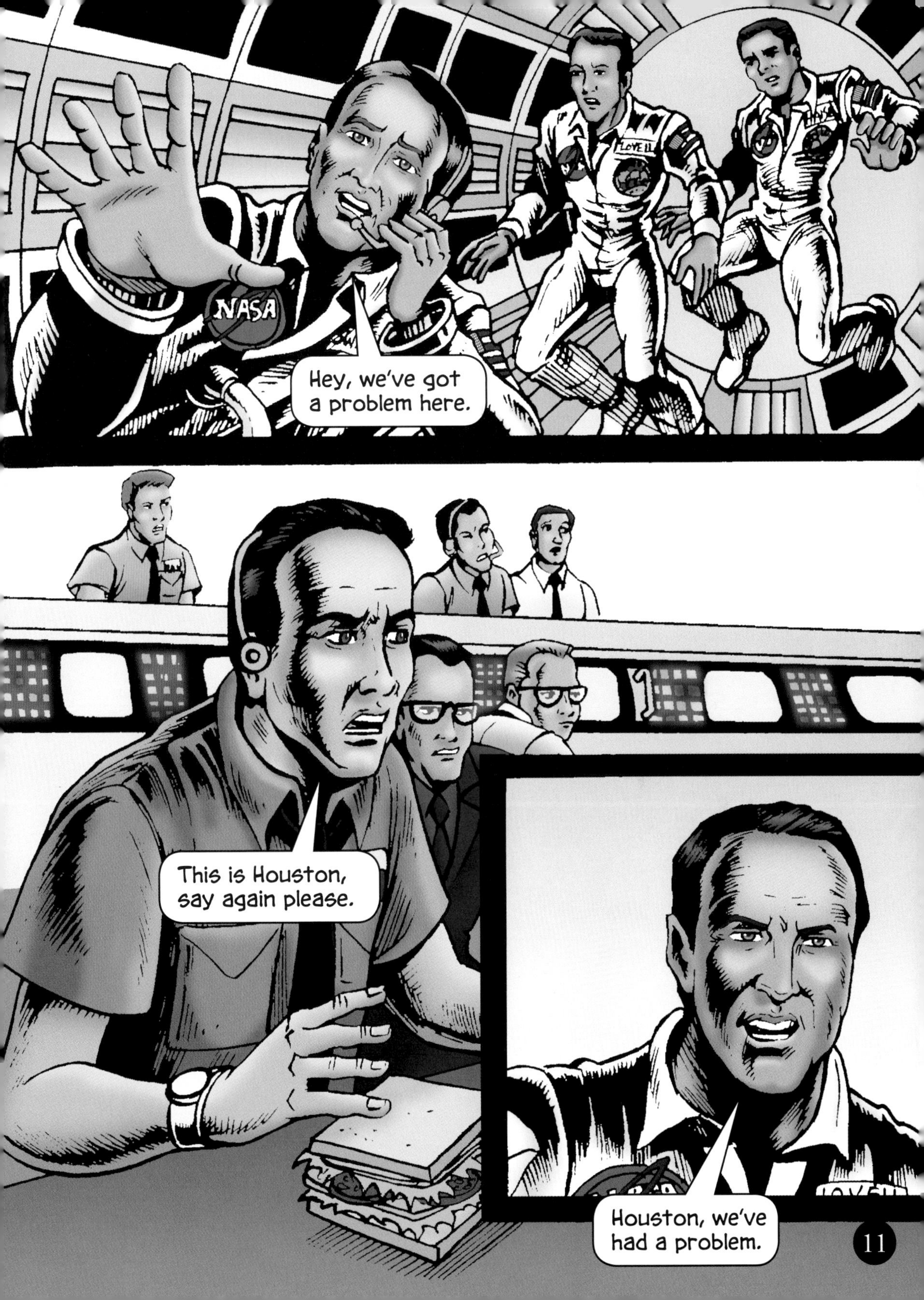
Hey, we've got a problem here.
This is Houston, say again please.
Houston, we've had a problem.

Chapter 2
Solving the Problem

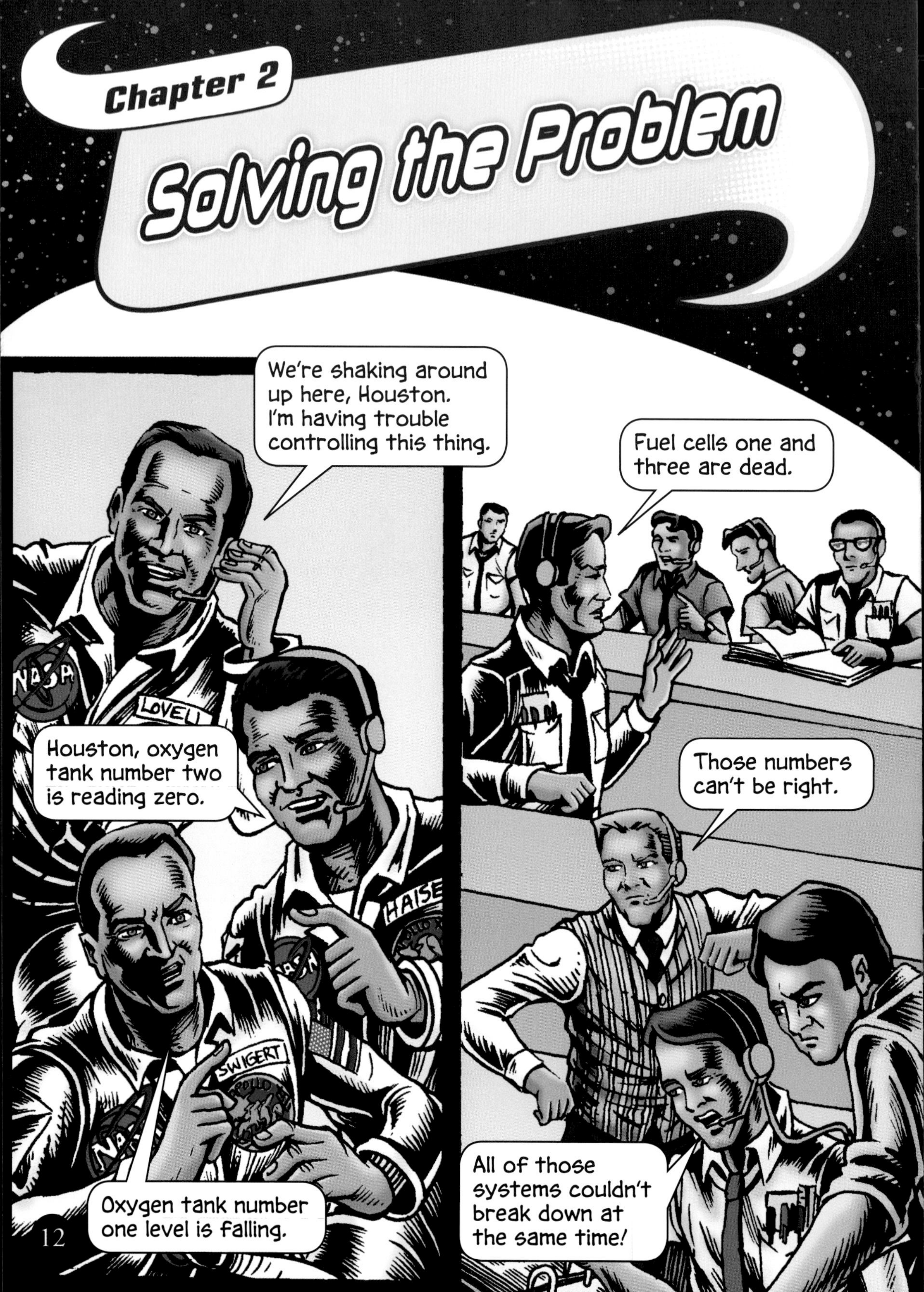
We're shaking around up here, Houston. I'm having trouble controlling this thing.
Houston, oxygen tank number two is reading zero.
Oxygen tank number one level is falling.
Fuel cells one and three are dead.
Those numbers can't be right.
All of those systems couldn't break down at the same time!

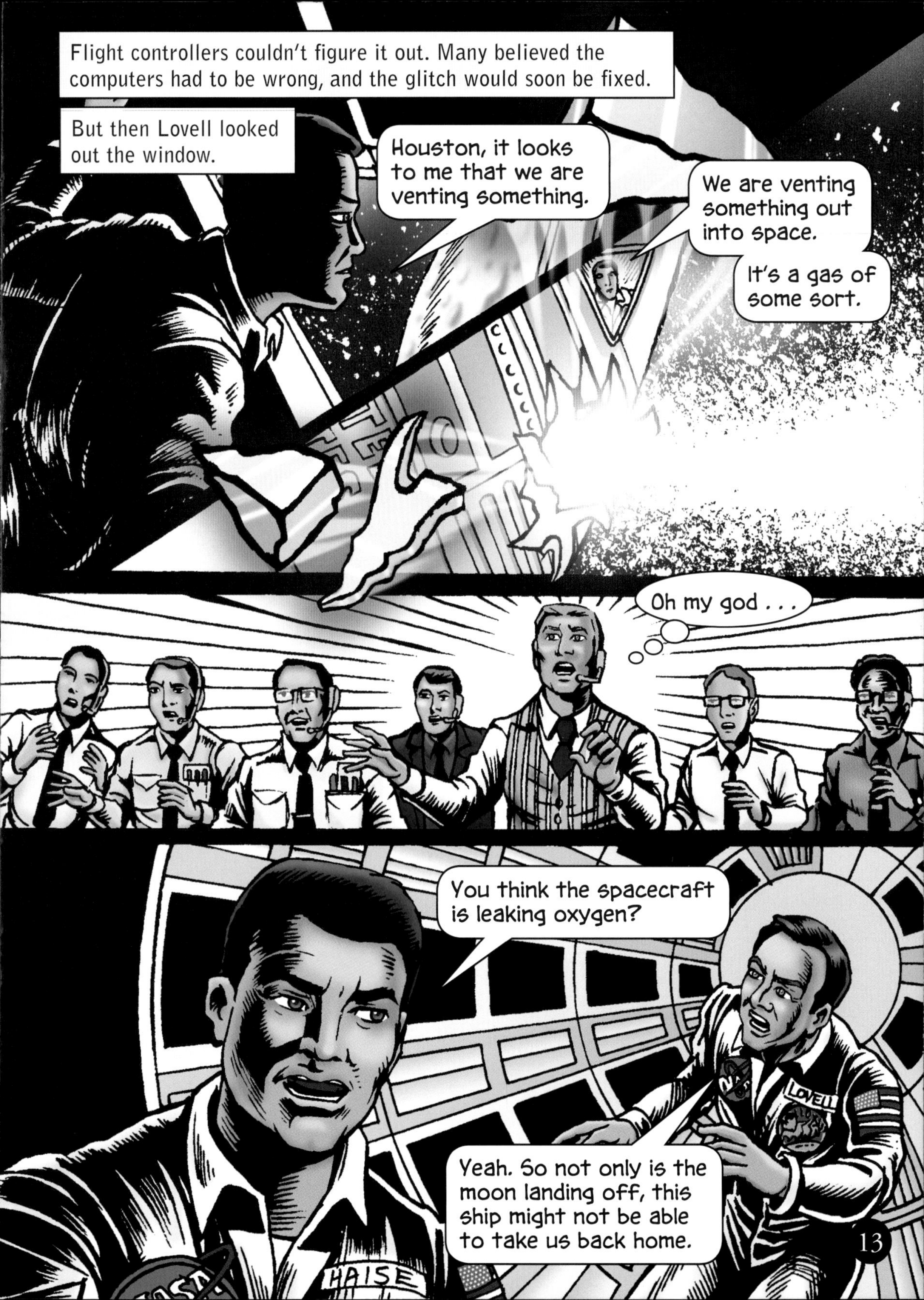
Flight controllers couldn't figure it out. Many believed the computers had to be wrong, and the glitch would soon be fixed.
But then Lovell looked out the window.
Houston, it looks to me that we are venting something.
We are venting something out into space.
It's a gas of some sort.
Oh my god . . .
You think the spacecraft is leaking oxygen?
Yeah. So not only is the moon landing off, this ship might not be able to take us back home.
LOVELL
HAISE

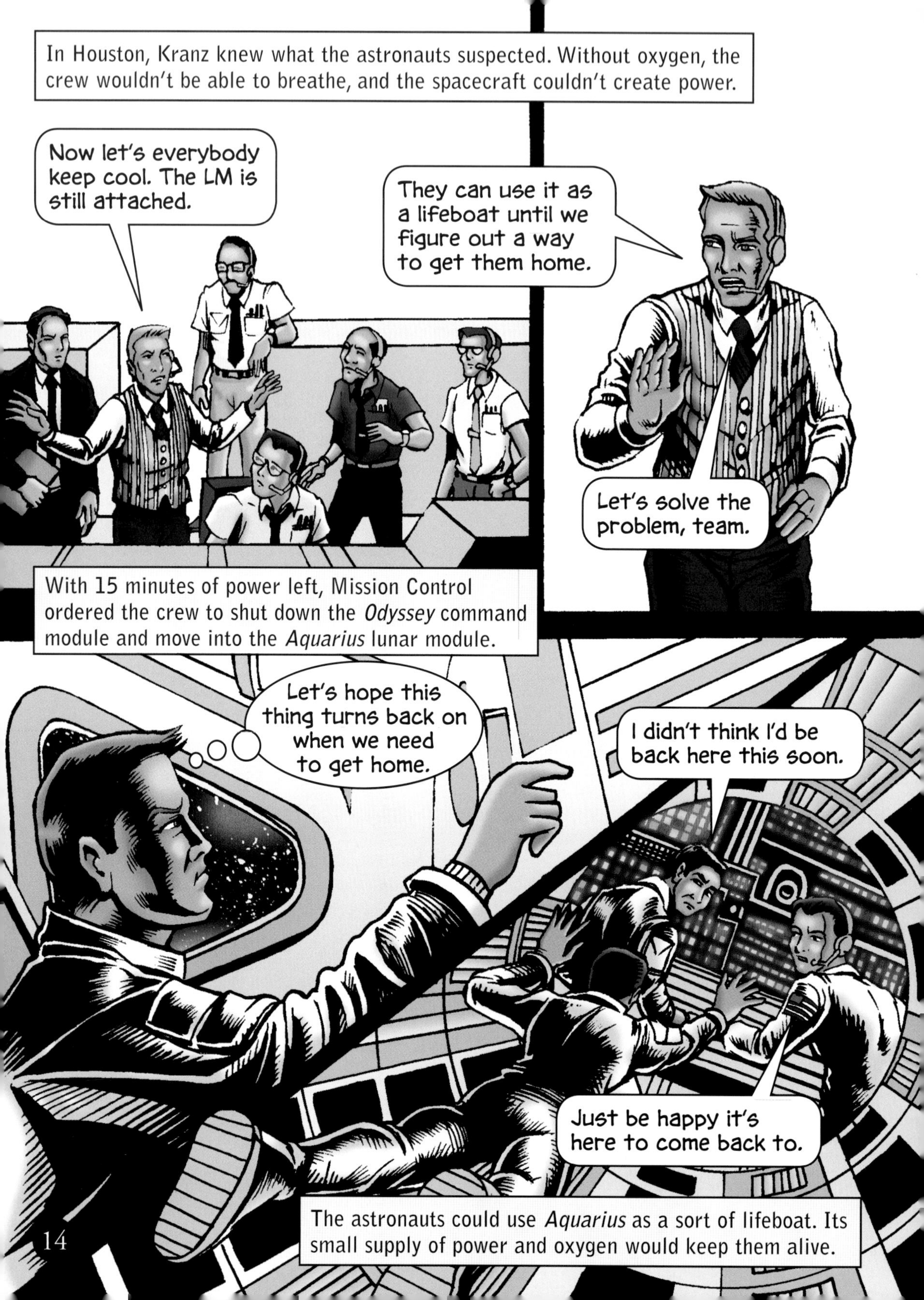
In Houston, Kranz knew what the astronauts suspected. Without oxygen, the crew wouldn't be able to breathe, and the spacecraft couldn't create power.
Now let's everybody keep cool. The LM is still attached.
They can use it as a lifeboat until we figure out a way to get them home.
Let's solve the problem, team.
With 15 minutes of power left, Mission Control ordered the crew to shut down the *Odyssey* command module and move into the *Aquarius* lunar module.
Let's hope this thing turns back on when we need to get home.
I didn't think I'd be back here this soon.
Just be happy it's here to come back to.
The astronauts could use *Aquarius* as a sort of lifeboat. Its small supply of power and oxygen would keep them alive.

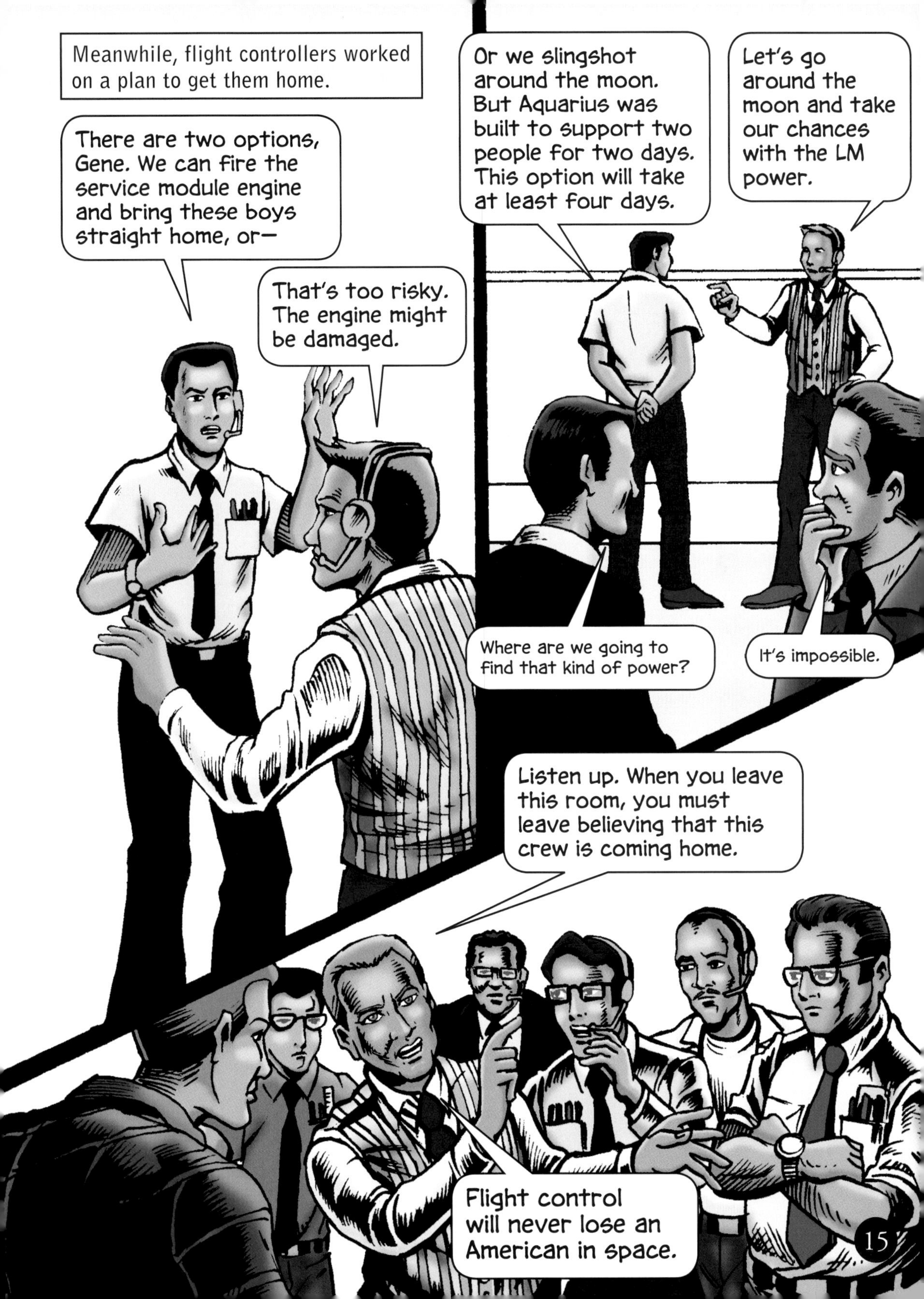

Meanwhile, flight controllers worked on a plan to get them home.
There are two options, Gene. We can fire the service module engine and bring these boys straight home, or—
That's too risky. The engine might be damaged.
Or we slingshot around the moon. But Aquarius was built to support two people for two days. This option will take at least four days.
Let's go around the moon and take our chances with the LM power.
Where are we going to find that kind of power?
It's impossible.
Listen up. When you leave this room, you must leave believing that this crew is coming home.
Flight control will never lose an American in space.

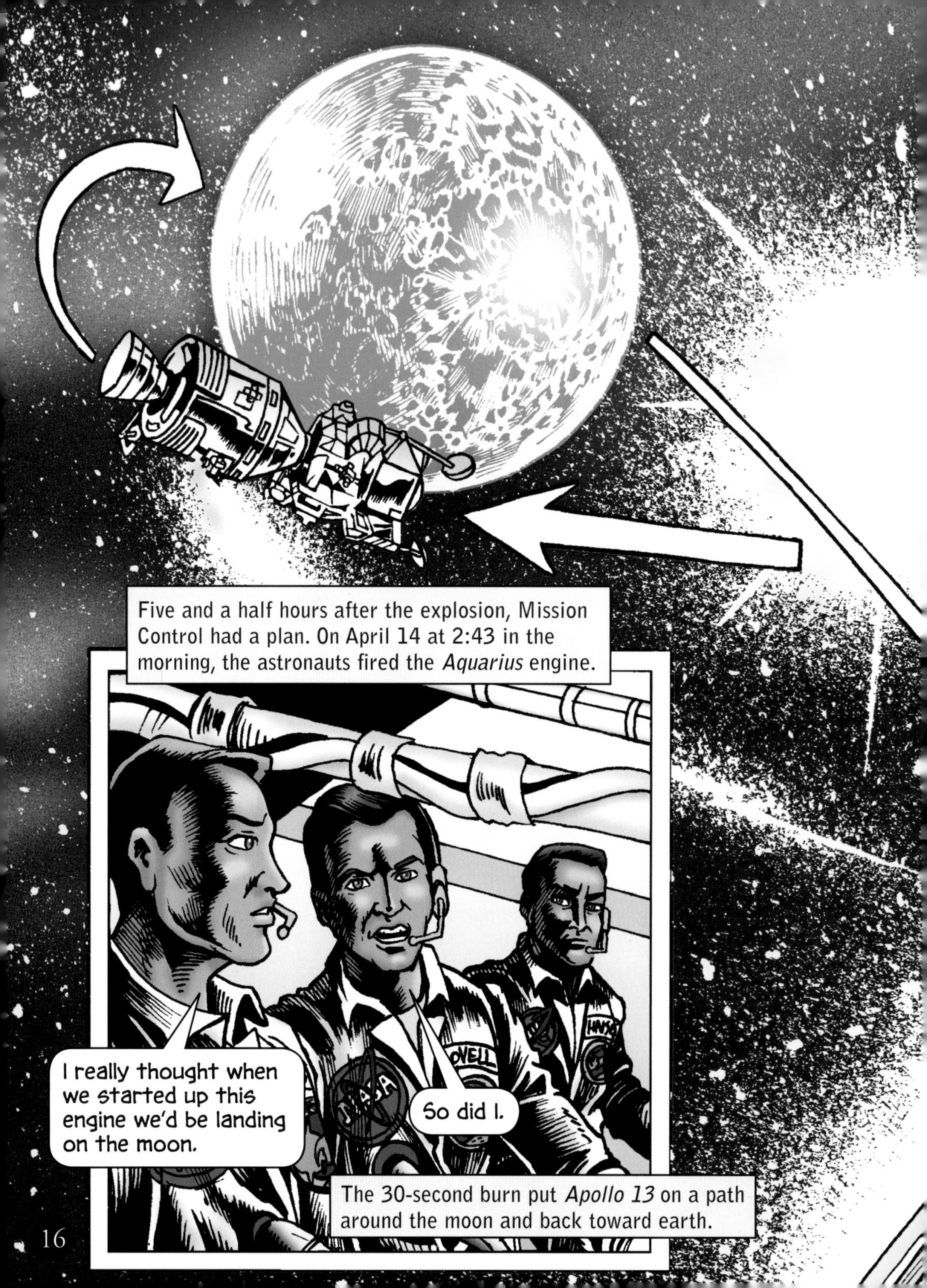
Five and a half hours after the explosion, Mission Control had a plan. On April 14 at 2:43 in the morning, the astronauts fired the *Aquarius* engine.
I really thought when we started up this engine we'd be landing on the moon.
So did I.
The 30-second burn put *Apollo 13* on a path around the moon and back toward earth.

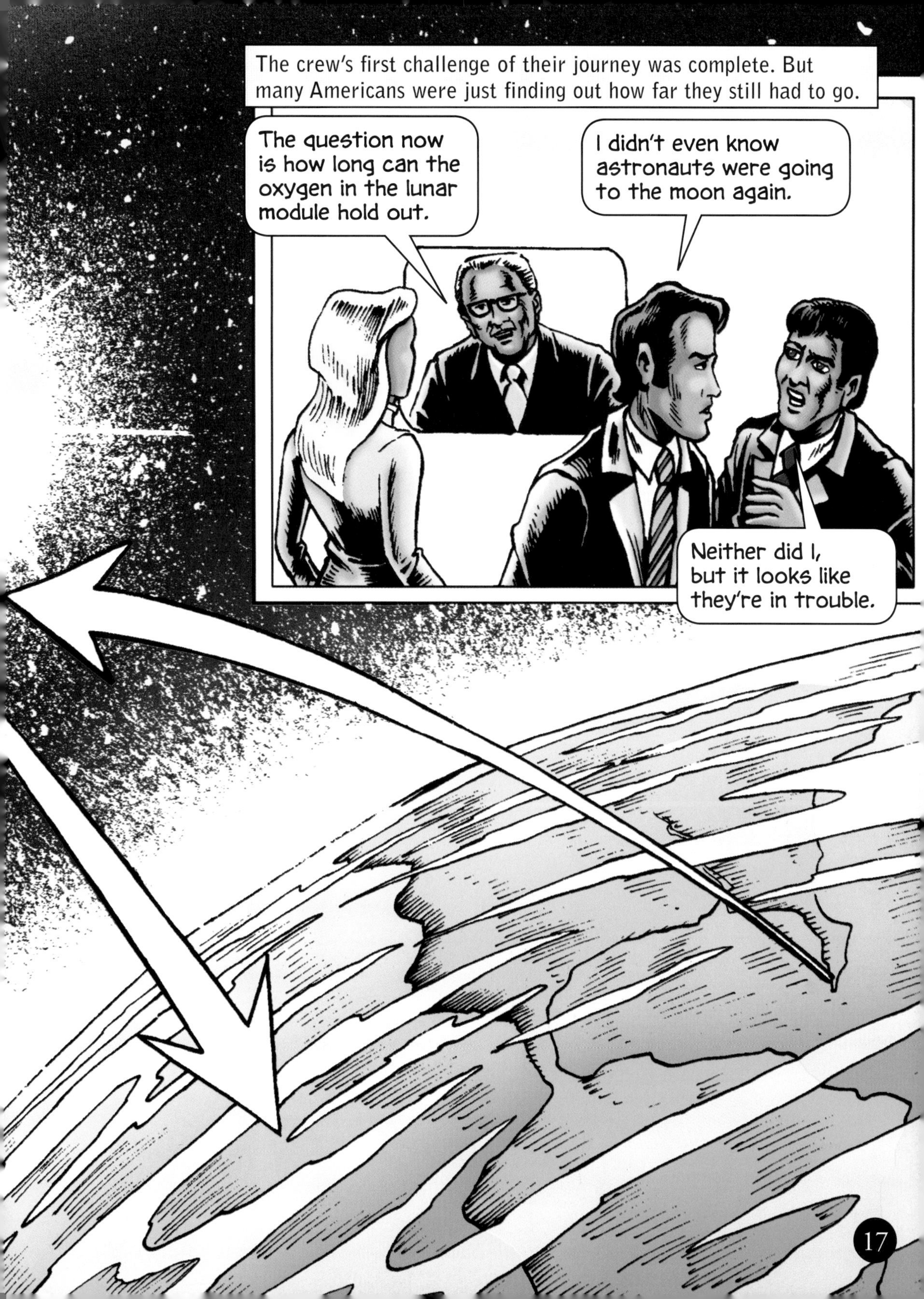
The crew's first challenge of their journey was complete. But many Americans were just finding out how far they still had to go.
The question now is how long can the oxygen in the lunar module hold out.
I didn't even know astronauts were going to the moon again.
Neither did I, but it looks like they're in trouble.

Chapter 3
The Long Journey Home

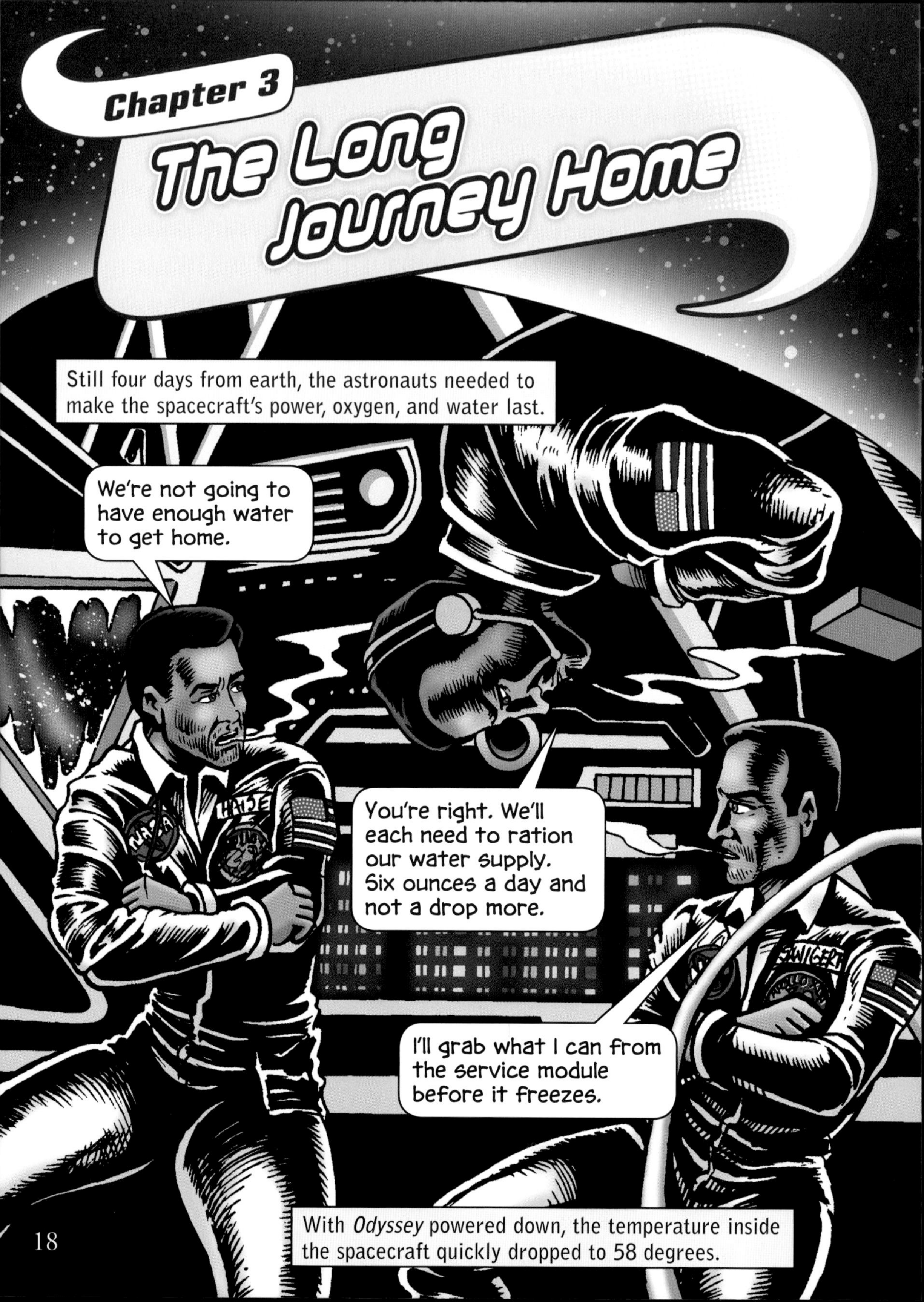
Still four days from earth, the astronauts needed to make the spacecraft's power, oxygen, and water last.
We're not going to have enough water to get home.
You're right. We'll each need to ration our water supply. Six ounces a day and not a drop more.
I'll grab what I can from the service module before it freezes.
With *Odyssey* powered down, the temperature inside the spacecraft quickly dropped to 58 degrees.

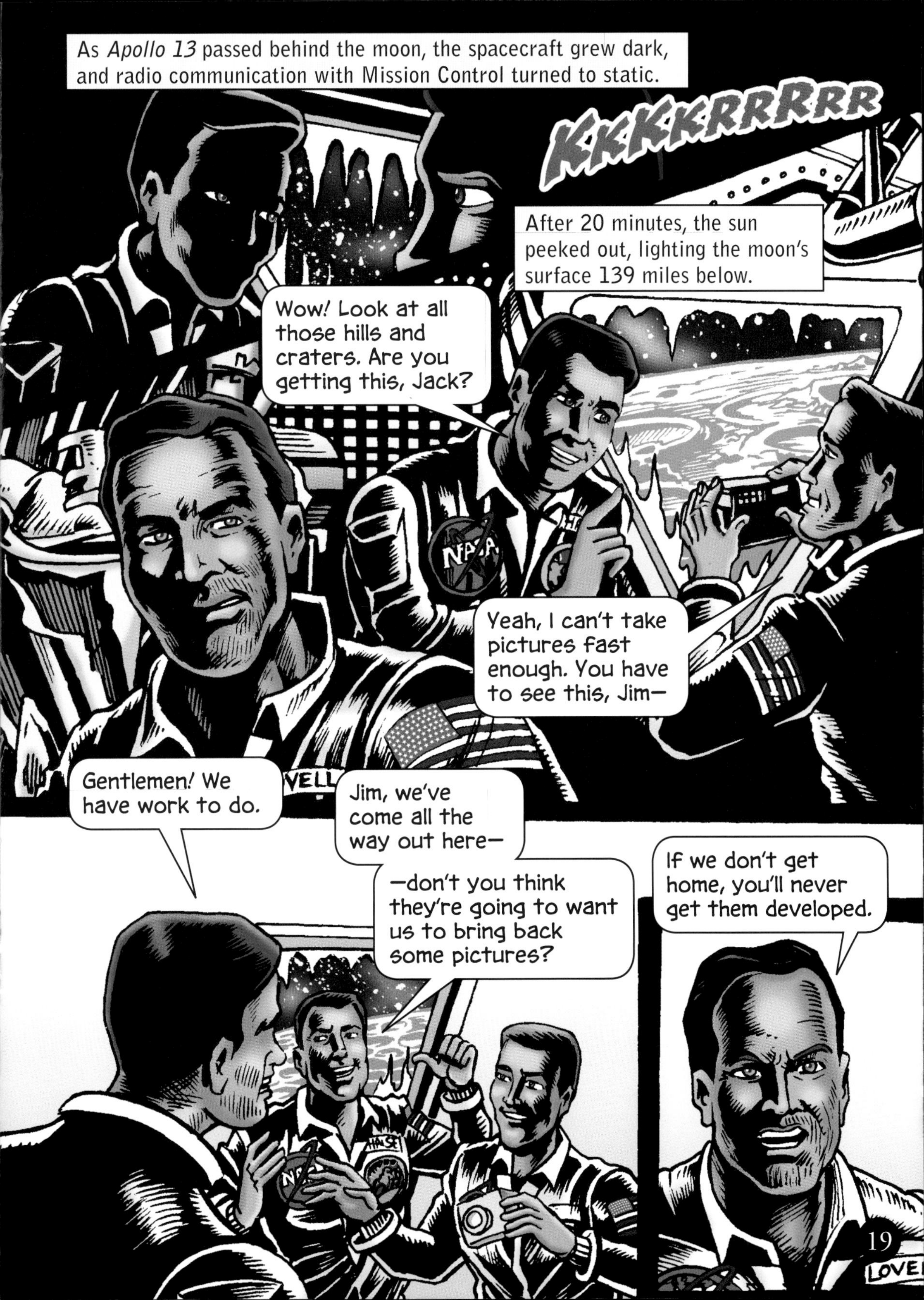
As *Apollo 13* passed behind the moon, the spacecraft grew dark, and radio communication with Mission Control turned to static.
KKKKKRRRRrr
After 20 minutes, the sun peeked out, lighting the moon's surface 139 miles below.
Wow! Look at all those hills and craters. Are you getting this, Jack?
Yeah, I can't take pictures fast enough. You have to see this, Jim—
Gentlemen! We have work to do.
Jim, we've come all the way out here—
—don't you think they're going to want us to bring back some pictures?
If we don't get home, you'll never get them developed.

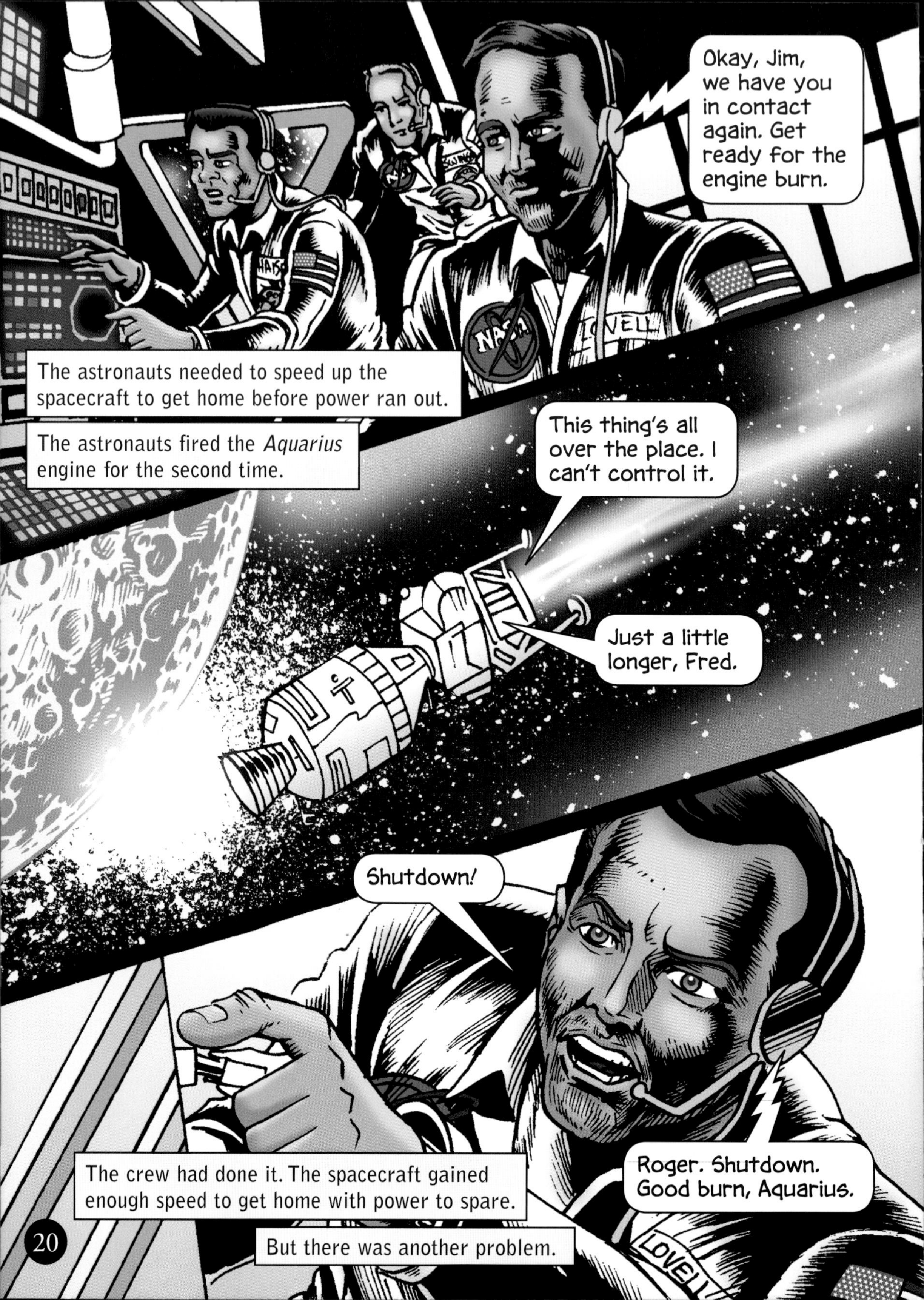
Okay, Jim, we have you in contact again. Get ready for the engine burn.
The astronauts needed to speed up the spacecraft to get home before power ran out.
The astronauts fired the Aquarius engine for the second time.
This thing's all over the place. I can't control it.
Just a little longer, Fred.
Shutdown!
Roger. Shutdown. Good burn, Aquarius.
The crew had done it. The spacecraft gained enough speed to get home with power to spare.
But there was another problem.

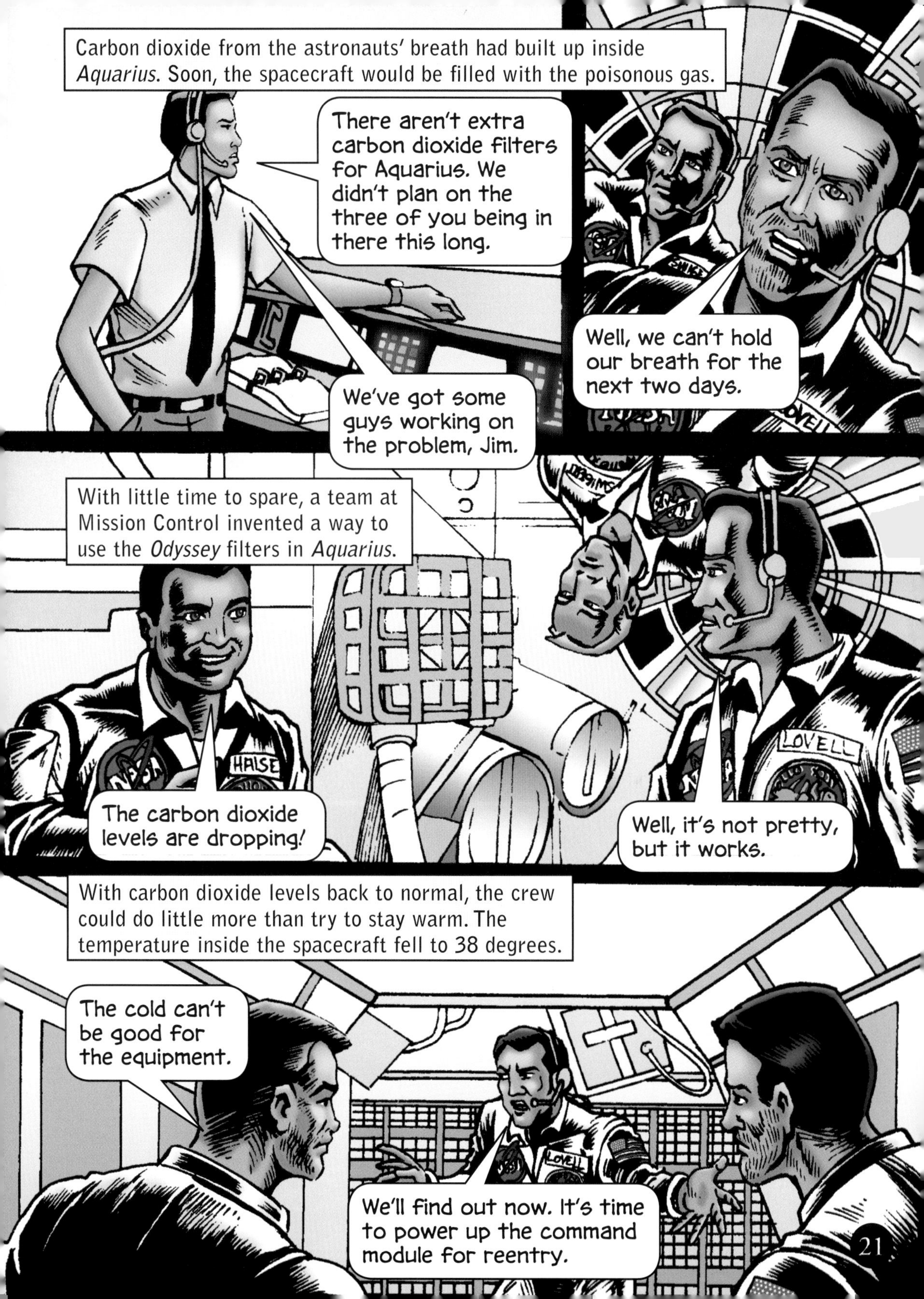

Carbon dioxide from the astronauts' breath had built up inside *Aquarius*. Soon, the spacecraft would be filled with the poisonous gas.
There aren't extra carbon dioxide filters for Aquarius. We didn't plan on the three of you being in there this long.
We've got some guys working on the problem, Jim.
Well, we can't hold our breath for the next two days.
With little time to spare, a team at Mission Control invented a way to use the *Odyssey* filters in *Aquarius*.
The carbon dioxide levels are dropping!
Well, it's not pretty, but it works.
With carbon dioxide levels back to normal, the crew could do little more than try to stay warm. The temperature inside the spacecraft fell to 38 degrees.
The cold can't be good for the equipment.
We'll find out now. It's time to power up the command module for reentry.

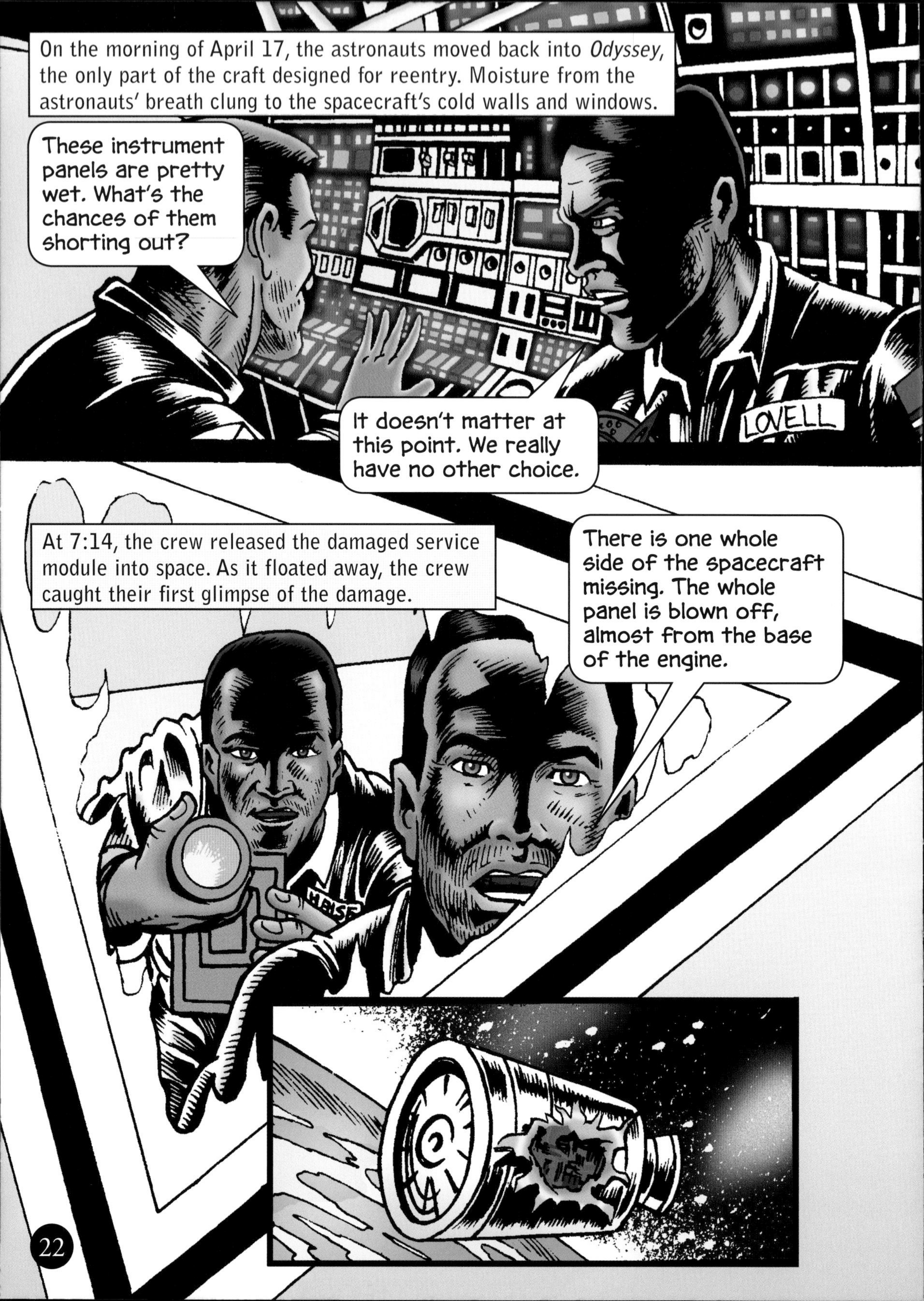
On the morning of April 17, the astronauts moved back into *Odyssey*, the only part of the craft designed for reentry. Moisture from the astronauts' breath clung to the spacecraft's cold walls and windows.
These instrument panels are pretty wet. What's the chances of them shorting out?
It doesn't matter at this point. We really have no other choice.
LOVELL
At 7:14, the crew released the damaged service module into space. As it floated away, the crew caught their first glimpse of the damage.
There is one whole side of the spacecraft missing. The whole panel is blown off, almost from the base of the engine.

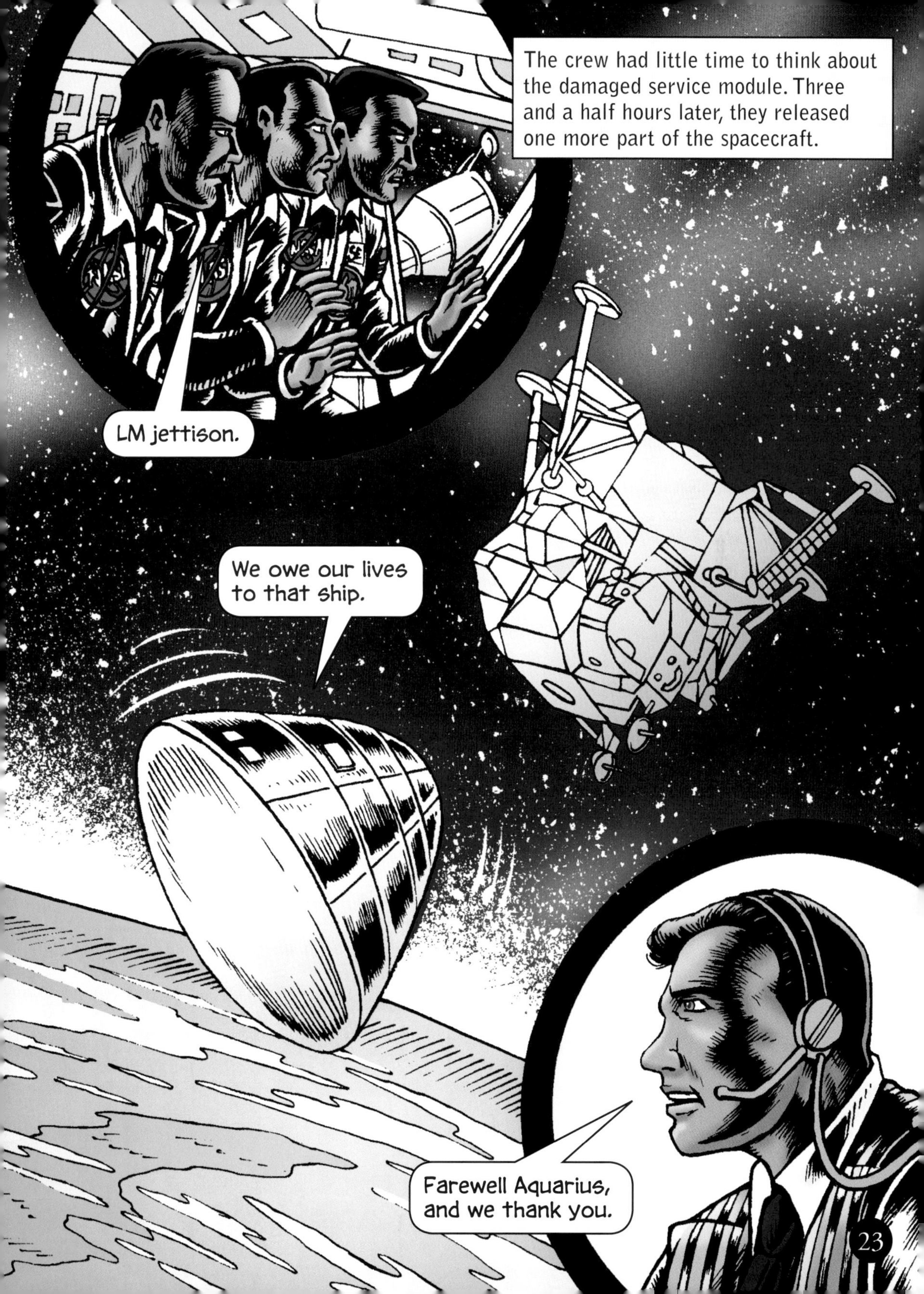
The crew had little time to think about the damaged service module. Three and a half hours later, they released one more part of the spacecraft.
LM jettison.
We owe our lives to that ship.
Farewell Aquarius, and we thank you.

Chapter 4
Splashdown

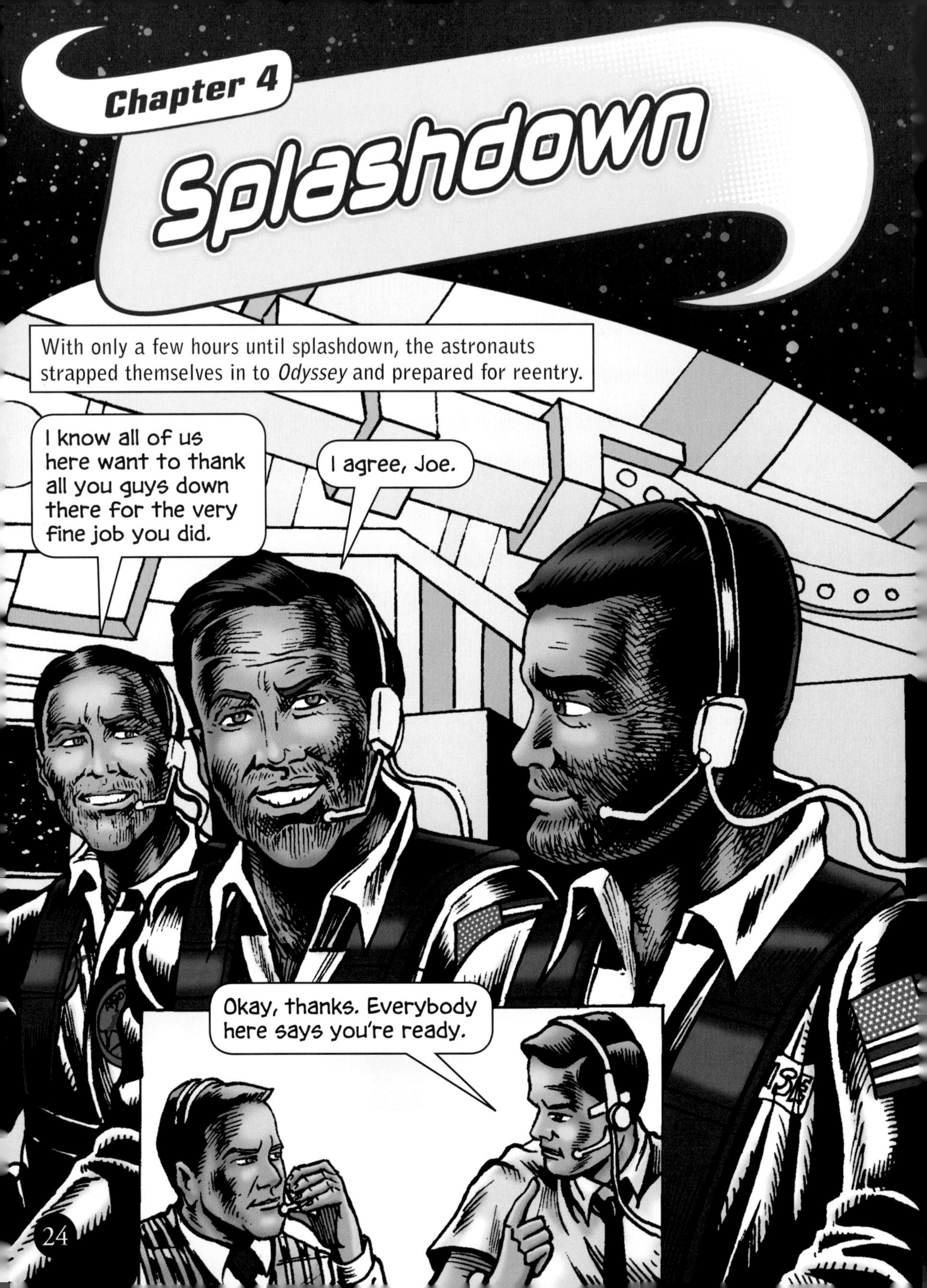
With only a few hours until splashdown, the astronauts strapped themselves in to *Odyssey* and prepared for reentry.
I know all of us here want to thank all you guys down there for the very fine job you did.
I agree, Joe.
Okay, thanks. Everybody here says you're ready.

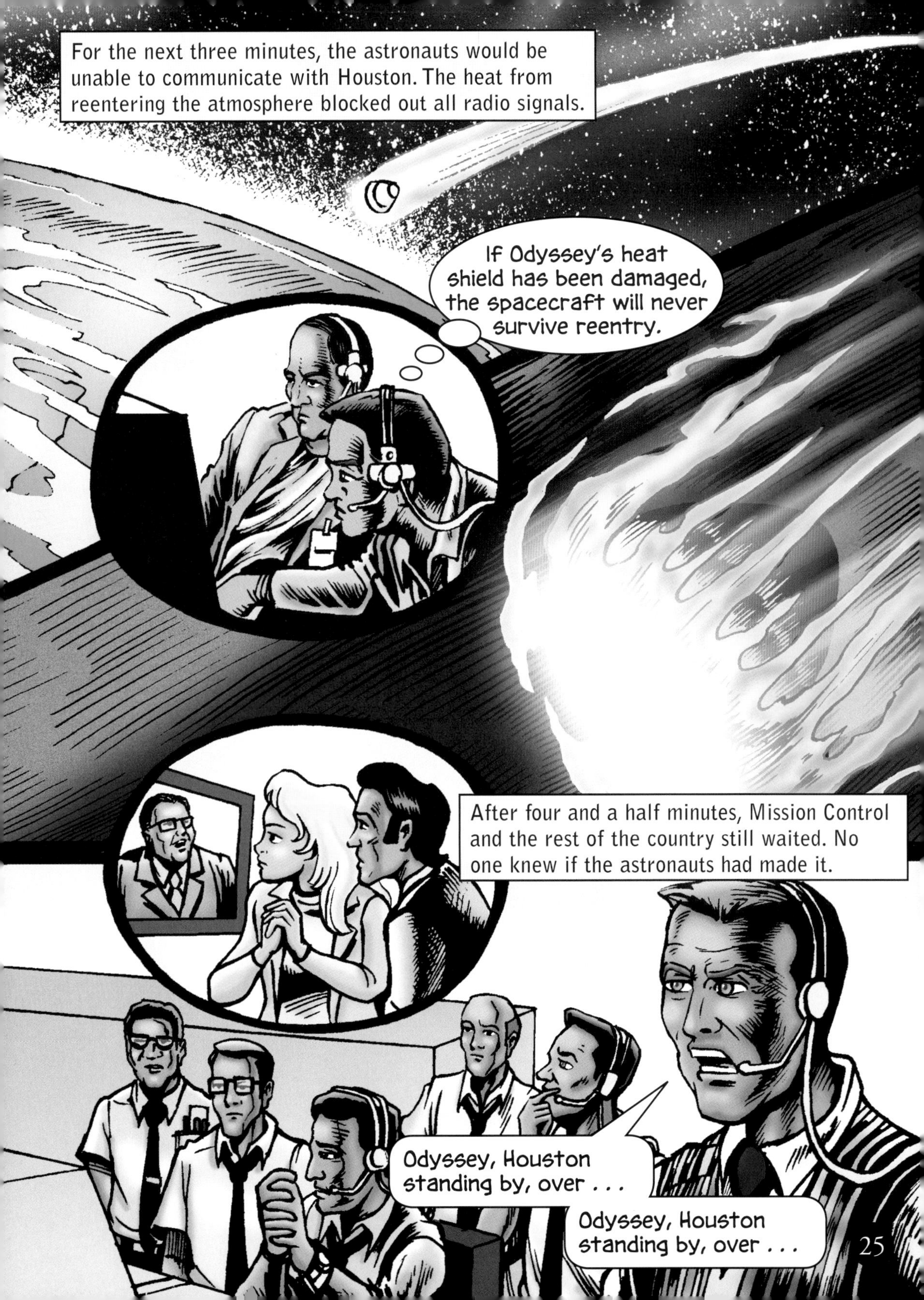
For the next three minutes, the astronauts would be unable to communicate with Houston. The heat from reentering the atmosphere blocked out all radio signals.
If Odyssey's heat shield has been damaged, the spacecraft will never survive reentry.
After four and a half minutes, Mission Control and the rest of the country still waited. No one knew if the astronauts had made it.
Odyssey, Houston standing by, over . . .
Odyssey, Houston standing by, over . . .

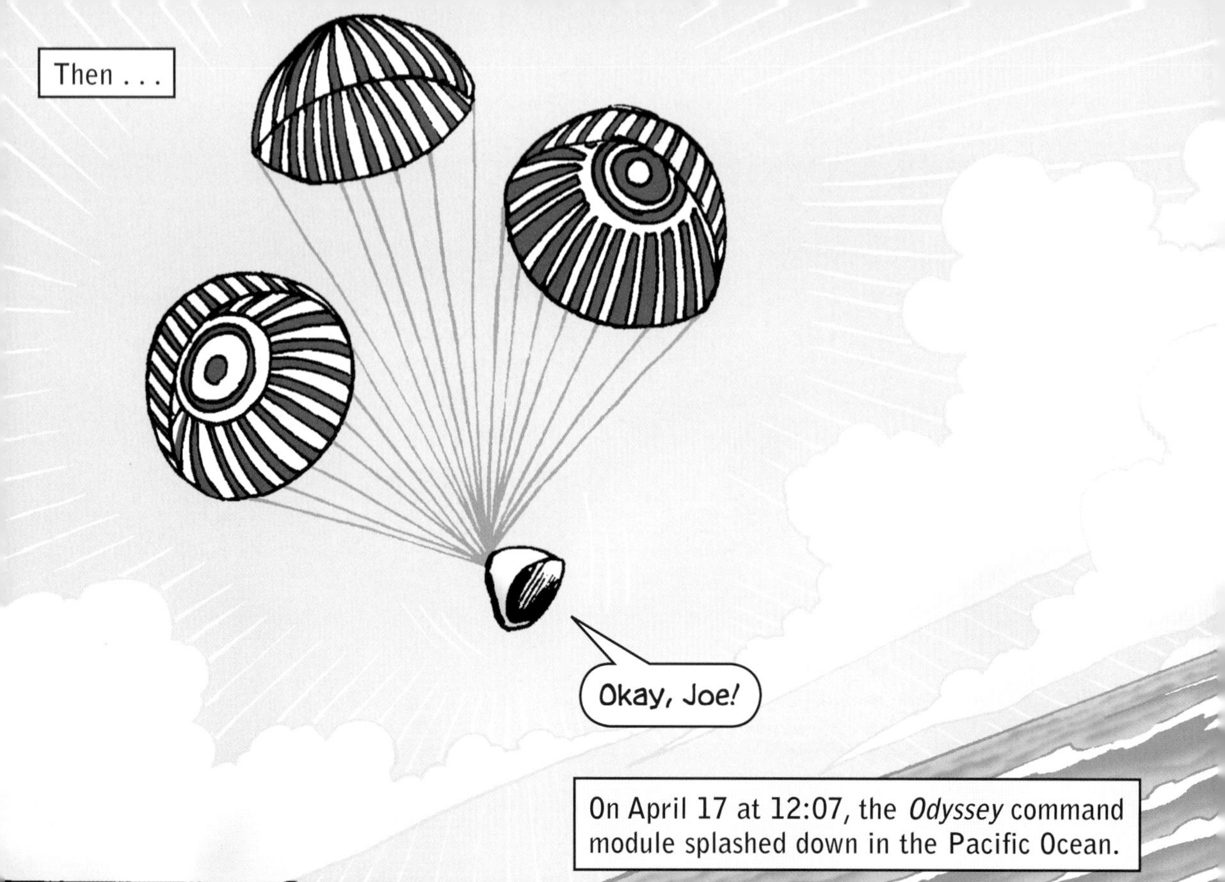
Then . . .
Okay, Joe!
On April 17 at 12:07, the *Odyssey* command module splashed down in the Pacific Ocean.

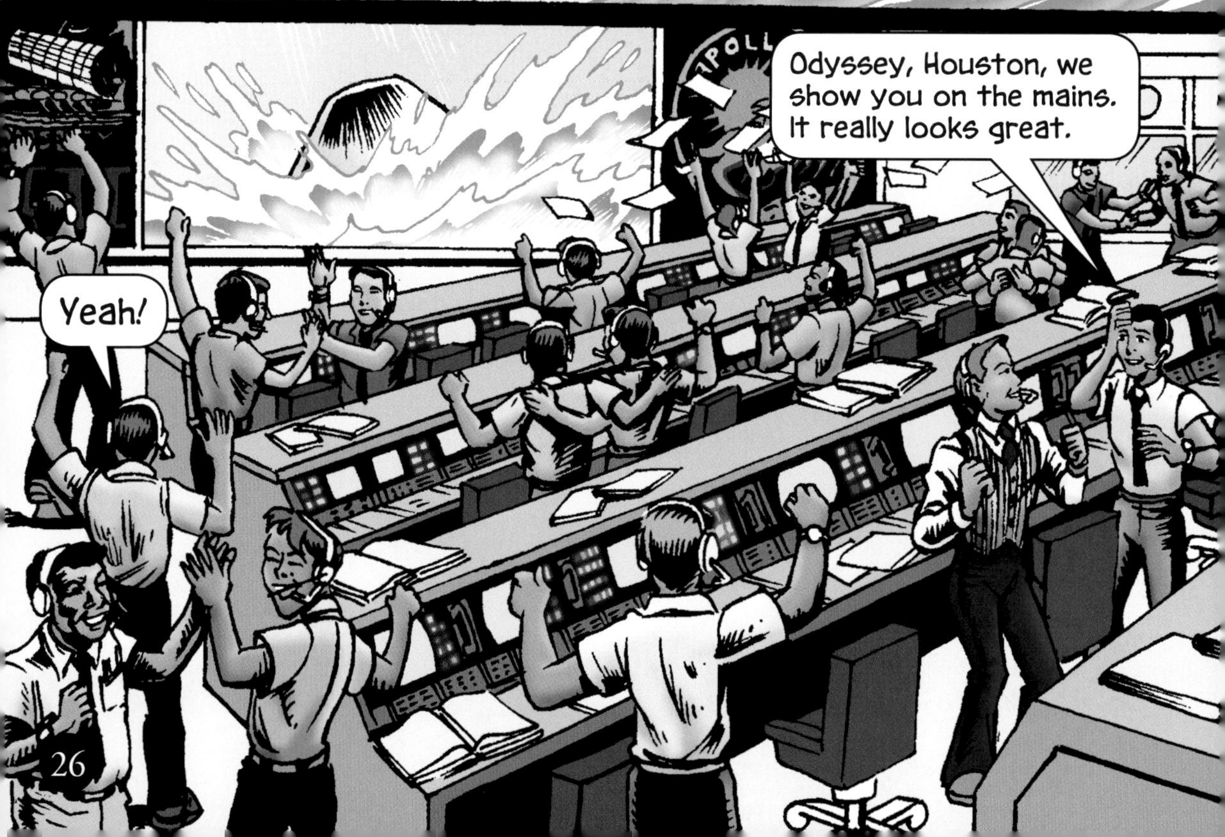
Odyssey, Houston, we show you on the mains. It really looks great.
Yeah!

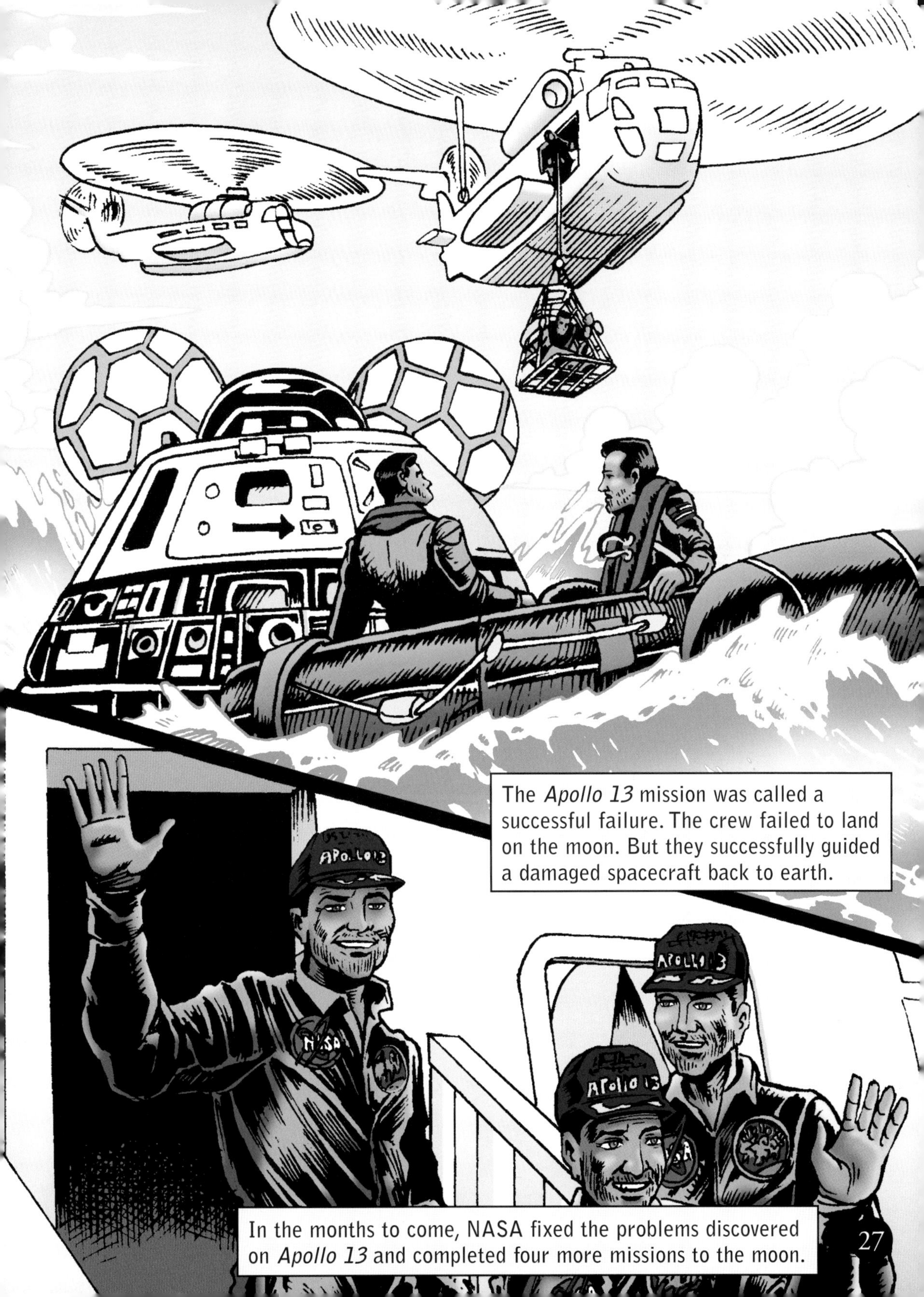
The *Apollo 13* mission was called a successful failure. The crew failed to land on the moon. But they successfully guided a damaged spacecraft back to earth.
In the months to come, NASA fixed the problems discovered on *Apollo 13* and completed four more missions to the moon.

More About Apollo 13

 Three days before the mission, Jack Swigert replaced astronaut Ken Mattingly as *Apollo 13* command module pilot. Mattingly had been exposed to an illness called the German measles. Doctors worried he would become sick while in space. Mattingly never got sick and helped flight controllers during the rescue mission.

 The Saturn V rocket launched all of the Apollo moon missions. It was the largest rocket ever used by NASA, standing 60 feet taller than the Statue of Liberty.

 Only five minutes after launch, the *Apollo 13* mission nearly ended. The first stage of the Saturn V had fallen off, and the second-stage engines were burning smoothly. Then suddenly, one of the engines shut down. Flight controllers at Mission Control acted quickly. They burned the remaining engines a little longer and saved the mission.

 The command module's display panel included 24 instruments, 40 indicators, 71 lights, and 566 switches.

- During the rescue, Lovell, Haise, and Swigert limited their drinking water. By the end of the mission, each member of the crew was severely dehydrated. Commander Jim Lovell lost nearly 14 pounds. The crew lost a total of 31.5 pounds during their nearly 6 days in space.

- On April 14, the U.S. Senate adopted a resolution asking for all businesses and media to join in prayer for the safety of the astronauts.

- After a long investigation, the *Apollo 13* Accident Review Board identified the cause of the explosion. Damaged wires shorted out and caught fire inside oxygen tank 2. Within seconds, the tank exploded. The explosion damaged oxygen tank 1 and part of the service module.

- The *Odyssey* command module of *Apollo 13* is on display at the Kansas Cosmosphere and Space Center in Hutchinson, Kansas. Visitors to the museum can view the vehicle that kept the astronauts alive during reentry.

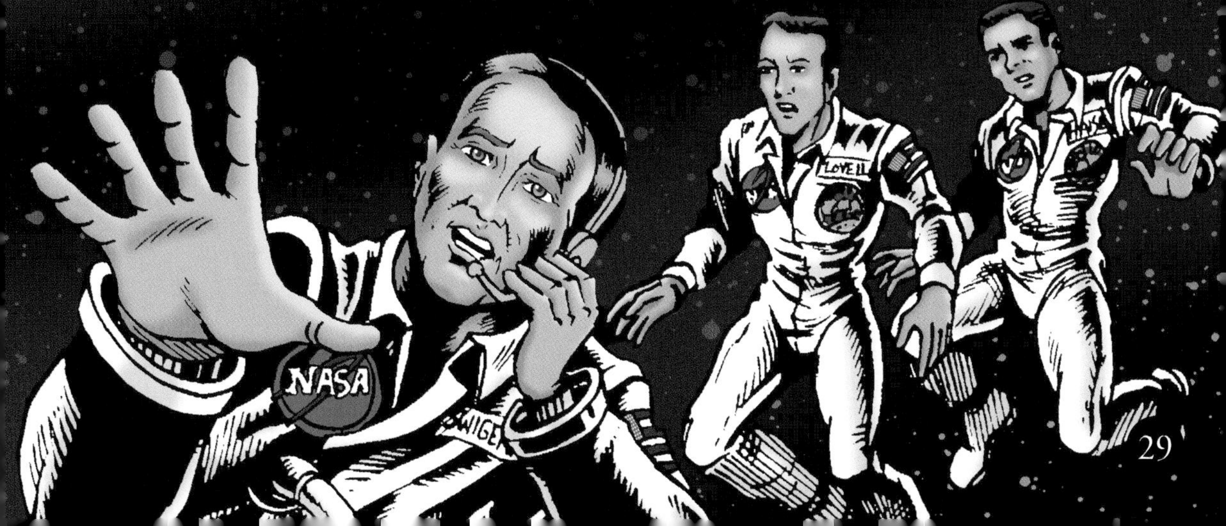
NASA
LOVELL

GLOSSARY

broadcast (BRAWD-kast)—a TV or radio program

Capcom (KAP-kom)—the flight control team on the ground that radios messages to the astronauts

carbon dioxide (KAR-buhn dye-OK-side)—a gas with no color or odor; people breathe this gas out.

jettison (JET-uh-suhn)—to throw out something that is no longer needed

module (MOJ-ool)—a separate section that can be linked to other parts

ration (RASH-uhn)—to give out in limited amounts

reentry (ree-EN-tree)—the return of a spacecraft through earth's atmosphere

splashdown (SPLASH-doun)—the landing of a spacecraft in the ocean

INTERNET SITES

FactHound offers a safe, fun way to find Internet sites related to this book. All of the sites on FactHound have been researched by our staff.

Here's how:

1. *Visit www.facthound.com*
2. Type in this special code **0736854762** for age-appropriate sites. Or enter a search word related to this book for a more general search.
3. Click on the **Fetch It** button.

FactHound will fetch the best sites for you!

READ MORE

Beyer, Mark. *Crisis in Space: Apollo 13.* Survivor. New York: Children's Press, 2002.

Graham, Ian. *You Wouldn't Want to Be on Apollo 13!: A Mission You'd Rather Not Go On.* New York: Franklin Watts, 2003.

Marcovitz, Hal. *Reaching for the Moon: The Apollo Astronauts.* Explorers of New Worlds. Philadelphia: Chelsea House, 2001.

Pierce, Alan. *Apollo 13.* American Moments. Edina, Minn.: Abdo, 2005.

BIBLIOGRAPHY

Apollo 13 PAO Mission Commentary Transcript. National Aeronautics and Space Administration. Johnson Space Center. http://www.jsc.nasa.gov/history/mission_trans/apollo13.htm

Cooper, Henry S. F. *Thirteen, the Apollo Flight that Failed.* Baltimore: Johns Hopkins University Press, 1995.

Godwin, Robert, ed. *Apollo 13: The NASA Mission Reports.* Burlington, Ont.: Apogee Books, 2000.

Kranz, Gene. *Failure Is Not an Option: Mission Control from Mercury to Apollo 13 and Beyond.* New York: Simon & Schuster, 2000.

Lovell, Jim, and Jeffrey Kluger. *Lost Moon: The Perilous Voyage of Apollo 13.* Boston: Houghton Mifflin, 1994.

INDEX